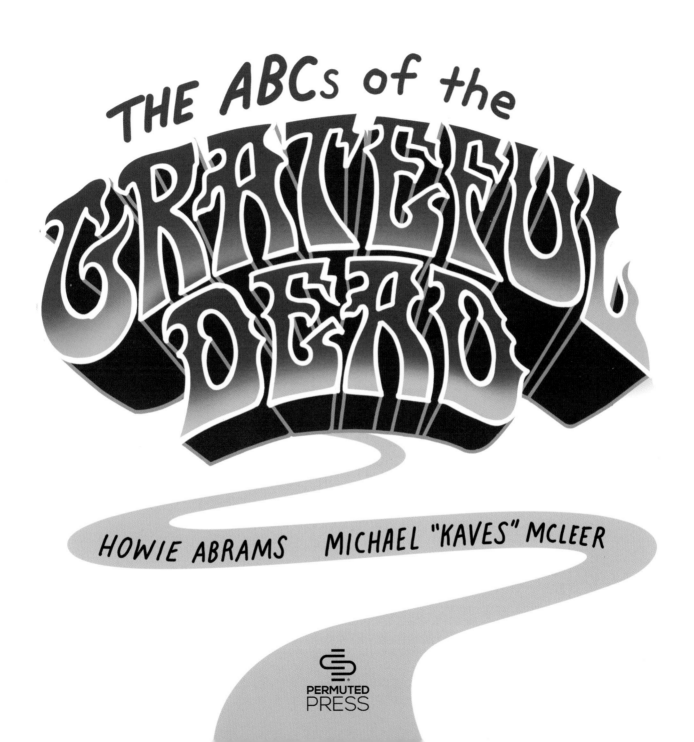

THE ABCs of the GRATEFUL DEAD

HOWIE ABRAMS   MICHAEL "KAVES" MCLEER

PERMUTED PRESS

Dedicated to
Nia, Ruby, Dylan, Quinn, Blaise,
Julie and Donna

A is for **American Beauty**,
A magnificent collection of songs.
Blending rock with folk and country sounds,
With plenty of sing-alongs.

GRATEFUL DEAD

B

is for Bears,
Dancing and grinning from ear to ear.
So furry and bursting with color,
Their joy is abundantly clear.

is for the **Carousel Ballroom**,
That turned into the Fillmore West.
The location of so many historic concerts,
It's impossible to say which was the best.

D is for Dead Heads,
The fans who follow the band on tour.
Singing, dancing, cheering and laughing,
Then calling out for more.

E is for Europe '72,
Recorded across the Atlantic sea.
Two albums of songs just wasn't enough,
Instead, they made three.

F

is for First,
As in the Grateful Dead's debut gig.
On December 4, 1965,
Who knew they'd get so big?

G is for Grateful,
Appreciating all that you've got.
Being thankful for the love that's all around,
If you've got love, you've got a lot.

is for **Haight and Ashbury**,
Cross streets in the San Francisco Bay.
Where a vibrant hippie lifestyle,
Shines brightly to this day.

ASHBURY
← 600

HAIGHT
← 1500

U.S. MAIL

NEWSPAPER

I is for Inducted,
To the Rock & Roll Hall of Fame.
Which the Grateful Dead were in 1994,
Forever immortalizing their name.

ROCK & ROLL

HALL OF FAME

GRATEFUL
DEAD

is for Jamming,
Which the band did on each song.
Extended with solos and funky strumming,
Until it's time to move along.

K

is for **Kindness**,
Being friendly and helpful every day.
Treating others with respect and affection,
That's the Grateful Dead way.

is for **Long Strange Trip**,
The history of our favorite band.
From the Warlocks to Dead & Company,
And all the places they've jammed.

DEAD HEAD

is for Miracle,
Someone's extra ticket to the show.
Gifted in line or in the parking lot.
Now, you're good to go!

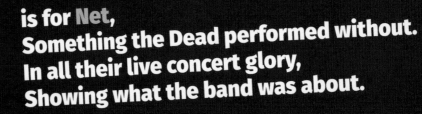

is for Net,
Something the Dead performed without.
In all their live concert glory,
Showing what the band was about.

is for the Orpheum Theatre,
Where the Dead played in '76.
Six glorious shows over seven beautiful nights,
Dead Heads dancing and getting their kicks.

P

is for Palo Alto,
In Spanish it means "tall tree."
It's where the Grateful Dead come from,
And where their spirit will always be.

Greetings from
PALO ALTO
California

DeadLands
OPEN SUN–FRI 5 PM
SATURDAY – OPENS 6 PM

MON 8PM	**PHIL LESH & FRIENDS**	$7
TUES 7PM	NYC APPEARANCE **RATDOG**	$10 PLUS GUEST
WED. 7PM	**THE OTHER ONES**	$7
THURSDAY 8PM	BACK BY POPULAR DEMAND **Furthur**	$5
FRI 9PM	**MICKEY HART BAND!**	$12

SOCK IT TO ME!!

is for The Q,
And all of the guys' other groups.
From RatDog, Furthur and the Mickey Hart Band,
Such incredible music troupes.

R

is for Recordings,
The cassettes of shows captured by fans.
In the taper's section behind the soundboard,
Then passed along hand to hand.

BUFFALO '77

A LONDON '72

S is for Space,
Which sets a dreamy atmosphere.
Breathtaking and dramatic,
With magical tones drifting through the air.

is for Terrapin,
Traveling to its happy place.
With a colorful tie-dye shell,
And a wide smile on its face.

U

is for **UC Santa Cruz**,
Where the Grateful Dead Archive is displayed.
With posters, and t-shirts and recordings,
Plus lots of the instruments they played.

UNIVERSITY OF CALIFORNIA
SANTA CRUZ

is for **Veggie Burritos**,
Sold in parking lots.
In exchange for miracles,
Served cold or piping hot.

is for Wall of Sound,
The Dead's massive speaker rig.
Ensuring Dead Heads could hear the band,
From the first note 'til the end of the gig.

is for Xylophone,
Melodious and sweet.
It appears in a couple of Grateful Dead songs,
Making each a musical treat.

Y

is for **Yippies**,
An often misunderstood bunch.
Whose members sought to change the world,
But whose parents thought they were out to lunch.

Z is for Zig-Zag,
As in zipping from here to there.
From the U.S., to Europe to the Middle East,
The Grateful Dead played everywhere.

Formed as a quintet in California in 1965, the Grateful Dead became as much a folktale as the story from which they drew their name. Fusing rock and roll, folk, and jazz with avant-garde, visual, and literary traditions--and virtually inventing a new way to play music in the process--they became one of the most popular, enduring, and influential bands in American history. Emerging as a vessel for a vibrant global counterculture, they would create an unparalleled original songbook through 30 years of recording and touring. Never playing the same setlist twice (except that once), the Dead's musical legacy remains unfathomably rich, spread across a combined body of live and studio recordings. Creating an artistic ecosystem all their own, the Grateful Dead would transform American music and arguably even America itself.

Howie Abrams

is a former music business executive turned author. He has co-created *The ABCs of Metallica, Finding Joseph I: An Oral History of H.R. from Bad Brains, Hip Hop Alphabet (One and Two), The Blood and the Sweat: The Story of Sick of It All's Koller Brothers* and others. He resides in New York City with his wife and teenage daughter.

Michael "Kaves" McLeer

is a legendary graffiti artist, the author of *Skin Graf: Masters of Graffiti Tattoo*, and illustrator for *The ABCs of Metallica*, *Hip-Hop Alphabet (One and Two)*. He has created logos and graphics for world renowned artists such as the Beastie Boys and brands the likes of Jaguar, Porsche, Audemars Piguet and Gretsch Guitars. He is an MC in the hip-hop/rock group Lordz of Brooklyn, and operates his art studio at Industry City in Brooklyn, the borough in which he resides with his wife and four children.

ACKNOWLEDGMENTS

Howie and Kaves wish to thank
Eleni Planet, Tonian Ortega and all at Rhino Records/Warner
Music Experience, Grateful Dead management,
Grateful Dead archivist and Legacy Manager David Lemieux,
Jacob Hoye and Permuted Press, David Wolpov, Julie Wolpov,
Beth Greenfield, Peter Nussbaum, Jamie Gardner, Bella Kozyreva,
Richard Idell, Scott Gerien, Jim Somoza, Donna McLeer,
and, of course, the Grateful Dead and Dead Heads everywhere

A PERMUTED PRESS BOOK
ISBN: 978-1-63758-661-7

The ABCs of the GRATEFUL DEAD

Cover and Interior Design by Donna McLeer / Tunnel Vizion Media LLC
Cover and Interior Illustrations by Michael "Kaves" McLeer
Additional Illustrations by Bella Kozyreva
Written by Howie Abrams

PERMUTED
PRESS

Permuted Press, LLC
New York • Nashville
permutedpress.com

Published in the United States of America